CONTENTS

GIVE IT A TRY!

It can take time to discover a sport that is right for you. The best way to find out if you will like a sport is to read about it, ask people about it, take a lesson or two, and give it a try!

All of the activities in this book can be dangerous. If you are trying a new activity, you should make sure that a skilled person is helping you. It is important to learn the basic safety rules and how to use the equipment correctly. If animals are involved, you must learn how to care for them.

This book is full of sports that you might like to try.

YOU CAN KAYAK AND CANOE!

Paddling a kayak or canoe can be easy and fun. It doesn't take long to learn the basic strokes and be able to stop and turn.

Because kayaks and canoes are light and can easily tip over, sooner or later you will probably capsize! It's a good idea to practice capsizing under supervision so when it happens, you will know what to do.

You should learn how to do an *Eskimo roll.* Then you can right yourself if you capsize.

NOW START EXPLORING!

Kayaks and canoes can be used on lakes, rivers, and oceans. Once you are experienced, you can enjoy the thrill of shooting *rapids,* surfing on waves, or simply exploring exciting new territories.

Talk the Talk

Bow: the front part of a boat

Stern: the back part of a boat

Eskimo roll: flipping right-side up after the kayak has turned upside down in the water

Rapids: swiftly moving stretches of water

Safety Tips

- Wear a life jacket.
- Let people know where you are going.
- Kayak and canoe in groups with experienced leaders.
- Practice capsizing with an experienced instructor.

YOU CAN RIDE HORSES!

You can learn how to ride and take care of a horse or pony by joining a horse club or riding school. At either of these places, you can learn how to bridle and saddle your horse, walk, trot, canter, change direction, and stop. You will also learn how to behave when you are around horses.

Riders communicate with their horses by using cues. These are given with the hands, legs, heels, and voice.

NOW START COMPETING!

After you have learned how to ride, you might want to start competing. You and your horse will need to work as a team. Together, you can take part in competitions such as dressage, jumping, and eventing.

Safety Tips

- Wear a helmet.
- Move quietly, and speak very calmly to your horse.
- Walk your horse the last stretch home so it can cool down.
- If you give your horse a treat, hold your hand flat so the horse doesn't confuse your fingers with the food.

Talk the Talk

Bit: the part of the bridle that fits into the horse's mouth

Schooling: training a horse for riding

Lame: when a horse has a leg injury and can't be ridden

Tack: riding equipment

YOU CAN RODEO!

Rodeo started when riders and ranchers had contests to see who was the best rider or calf roper. Wild horses were tamed and trained for riding. When a rider broke a horse, the horse would jump around and try to buck the rider off. From this ranch job came the bareback bronco riding of today's rodeo events.

Safety Tips

- Take lessons and practice before entering a competition.
- Never stand in front of a gate that rodeo horses are using. They move very fast, and you could get run over.
- Be careful at all times around rodeo animals.
- Never go inside a rodeo ring or corral unless you are supposed to be there.

Rodeo is a sport in which riders show their skills for riding and roping horses and cattle. There are events for children as well as adults.

Talk the Talk

Bronco: an untamed horse
Busting: training an untamed horse
Chutes: the pens you wait in before the event begins
Rigging: the equipment a rider holds onto when riding a bull or horse during an event

YOU CAN LEARN ROCK CLIMBING!

You can learn rock climbing at an indoor rock gym. Professional teachers can show you how to use the special equipment. You can also learn the commands to give the person who is climbing with you.

It is important to plan your climb. You need to know where you are going, and how to get back down the rock face.

NOW TRY RAPPELING!

Rappeling is a controlled descent down a rock face. You use a doubled rope that is coiled around your body and fixed either at the top, or at a higher point, of the rock face.

Once you have learned how to climb and rappel indoors, you will be ready to take your skills outside.

Safety Tips

- Climb with an experienced person.
- Climb with a rope and safety gear.
- Plan your climb.
- Have all equipment checked for safety before you climb.

Talk the Talk

Belay: to fasten a rope to a fixed object

Bolts: metal nuts used to anchor the rope to the rock face

Carabiner: the metal clip used to attach you to the rope

Harness: special nylon rope belts that wrap around a person's legs and waist, and attach to the belay rope

YOU CAN SAIL!

Many yacht clubs have small sailing boats and offer lessons on how to sail. You can start by sailing alone in smaller boats. Eventually, you can move on to larger boats, where you can sail with a team of people. Whatever their size, all sailing boats follow three basic principles of sailing.

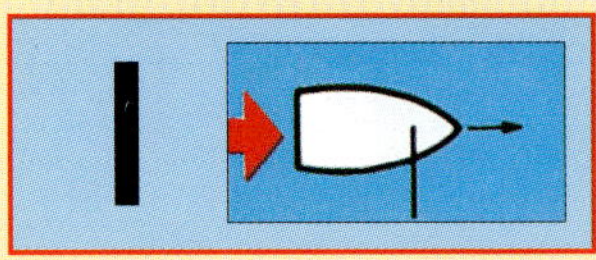

Wind hits a wide-spread sail from behind and simply pushes the boat along. This is *running downwind,* or *running before the wind.*

2

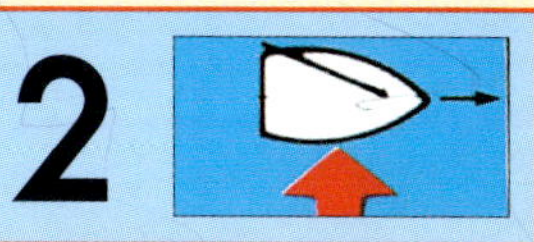

Wind hits a gently curved sail from the side, and the boat is both pulled and pushed by the wind. This is called *reaching,* the fastest kind of sailing.

3

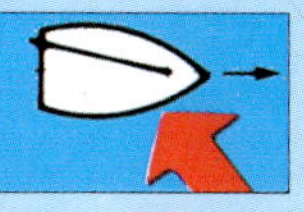

Wind hits a tightly curved sail from ahead, and the boat is pulled forward into the vacuum ahead of the sail. This is *sailing on the wind,* or *sailing close hauled.*

NOW PRACTICE CAPSIZING!

Even the best sailors capsize sometimes, so it is a good idea to practice getting back into a capsized boat with an adult helper. Then you'll know what to do if it happens to you.

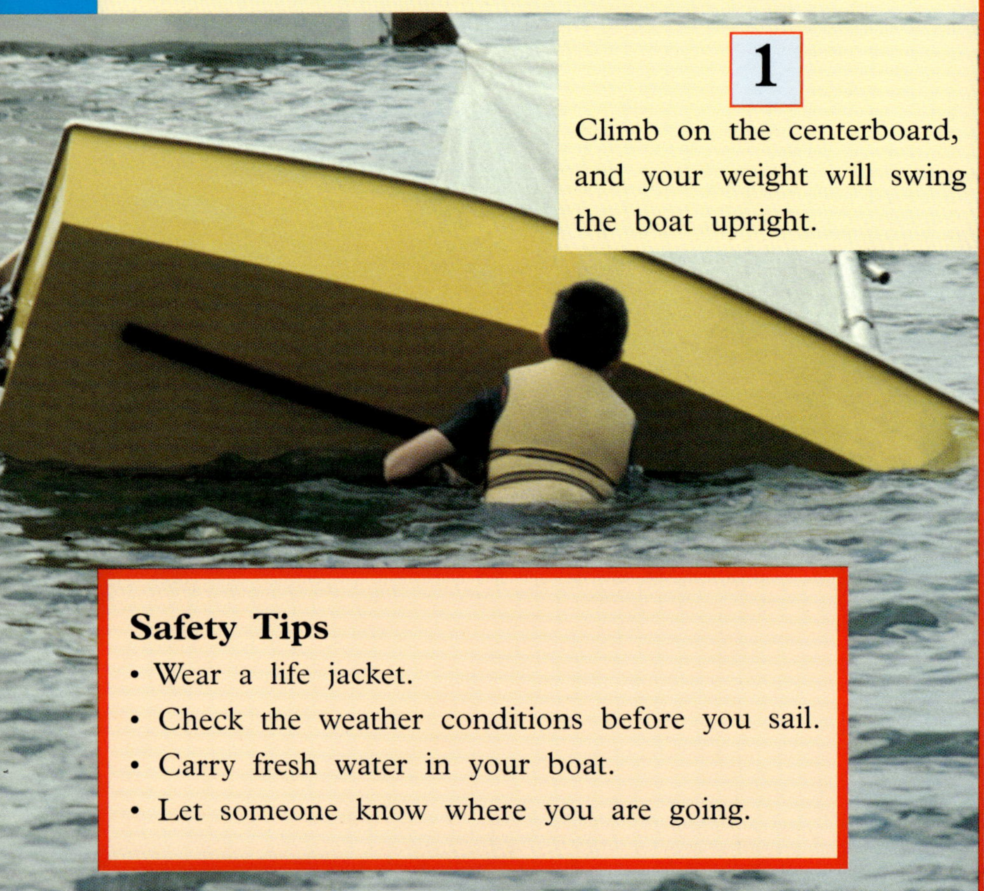

1

Climb on the centerboard, and your weight will swing the boat upright.

Safety Tips

- Wear a life jacket.
- Check the weather conditions before you sail.
- Carry fresh water in your boat.
- Let someone know where you are going.

2

Climb back in over the windward side or stern (rear end of the boat).

3

Start bailing!

Talk the Talk

Heel: to tip or tilt the boat

Starboard: the right-hand side of the boat

Port: the left-hand side of the boat

Come about!: a spoken signal to prepare for changing direction

YOU CAN BE A GYMNAST!

Gymnastics is a mixture of different events demonstrating strength, agility, coordination, and balance.

You can learn the skills of tumbling and gymnastics by joining a club where there are experienced instructors and safe equipment.

Safety Tips

- Practice new moves with a *spotter.*
- Warm up before exercising.
- Learn how to land and fall safely.
- Practice with the proper equipment and safety nets.

Talk the Talk

Aerial: a move completed in mid-air

Crash pad: a soft safety mat used during practice

Spotter: a person who helps you complete a move

Grips: guards worn on the hands

YOU CAN LEARN MARTIAL ARTS!

Martial arts were started in the Far East as combat sports. Today most people study martial arts as a form of exercise for both the body and the mind. It is also practiced as a form of self-defense.

You can learn many different kinds of martial arts; each one has different moves and aspects that make it unique. To find out more, you could contact your local *dojo*.

Safety Tips

- Have an instructor present if you are trying new moves.
- Don't tuck your thumb into your closed fist.
- Warm up before beginning to exercise.
- Wear protective pads when sparring.

Talk the Talk

Black belt: a belt worn by an expert in martial arts
Dojo: a place where you go to study martial arts
Tori: in judo, the defender
Sensei: a teacher or instructor in karate

YOU CAN SWIM!

It is very important to learn how to swim. If you can swim, you can learn to dive, surf, and body surf. You will feel confident in and around the water. You could even go on to represent your country at international sporting events.

Safety Tips

- Never dive into shallow water or into creeks or lakes that you don't know well.
- Tell an adult where you are swimming.
- At the beach, swim between the flags, and pay attention to the lifeguards.
- If you get tired, get out of the water.

Talk the Talk

Medley: a swimming competition in which a different stroke is used for each section of a race

Pike position: a diving position in which you bend forward and keep your legs straight

Shredder: a good surfer

Wipe out: to fall off a surfboard

YOU CAN START IN-LINE SKATING!

In-line skating is a combination of roller skating and ice skating. You wear skates that have three, four, or five wheels that are all in a straight line. In-line skating is a great way to keep fit. You can also learn how to play roller hockey.

Before you start in-line skating, make sure you are wearing a helmet, protective pads, wrist guards, and gloves.

Safety Tips

- Be sure that there is no traffic where you are skating.
- Wear protective gear.
- Always skate at a safe speed.
- Observe all traffic rules.

Talk the Talk

Extreme skating: the fancy, tricky skating that uses jumps, spins, and stunts

Facemask: the protective face cage on a helmet that should be worn at all times when playing roller hockey

Sidesurfing: to glide with the heels of both skates facing one another

Swizzle: when you move your skates on and off their edges

INDEX

FROM THE AUTHOR

I have always enjoyed sports. I especially like sports in which I can explore nature, like rock climbing and sailing.

When I was a child, I learned every new sport possible. Now, my children are old enough to start learning sports. It is fun to watch them try new things.

Sports take concentration, discipline, and determination. But most of all, sports are a blast!

DIANA SHORT YURKOVIC

Imagine That!

Fuzz and the Glass Eye
Which Way, Jack?
The Wish Fish
Famous Animals
Pie, Pie, Beautiful Pie
My Word! How Absurd
You Can Canoe!
A World of Imagination

Written by **Diana Short Yurkovic**
Photography by **Suzanne Dickens:** (pp. 10-11); **Jeff Evans:** (p. 23; p. 25; p. 28); **Hedgehog House:** (canoeing, cover; canoeing, pp. 6-7); **Richard Hoit:** (p. 17); **Sarah Irvine:** (gymnast, cover; horseback riding, p. 3; pp. 8-9; pp. 14-15; p. 22; and p. 24); **William Kaufman:** (rodeo, cover; pp. 12-13); **Legend Photography:** (kayaker, p. 3; p. 5; p. 7); **David Lowe:** (title page; p. 4; pp. 18-21; p. 27; pp. 30-31); **Marine Education and Recreation Centre:** (boy rappeling, cover and p. 16); **N.Z. Picture Library:** (girl surfing, p. 26); **Photosport:** (diver, p. 26); **Stock Photos:** Tom and Dee Ann McCarthy (roller hockey, cover and p. 2; p. 29)

05 04 03 02 01 00 99
10 9 8 7 6 5 4 3 2 1

Published in the United States by

a division of Reed Elsevier Inc.
500 Coventry Lane
Crystal Lake, IL 60014

Printed in Hong Kong
ISBN: 0-7901-1872-6